WHAT DO I DO... WHEN MOMMY IS GONE?

Prompted and Freeform Journal

Prompts By

Tanika J. West-Moore
"The Counseling Chef"

This journal is to accompany the "Adult's" Children's Book

and is

gifted to you:

_____

By

_____

who just wants to say:

_____

_____

_____

_____

_____

_____

_____

Catherine Harris ~ Sadie Russell ~ Linda Kay Morrison Thompson ~ Dearie J. Coleman ~ Mary Smith ~ Tirza Case

Dedicated to :

First and foremost the QUEEN!!

Adonia Mayette Smith–West MacGoodwin –Smith –West

(inside joke),

My Mother–In Love

Jean Moore,

My God –Mother

Thelma Battle Buckner,

And to my "sister, from another mister"

Adrianne R. Price.

Then, to all of my friends and family who have lost their mothers,

or mother figures. Be they men , women, boys , or

girls. A mother is a very hard thing to lose,

NO MATTER what, and no matter TO WHAT!!!!

Cherish them while you have them!!!!!

Love Always,

Tanika

Eva Pearl Walker ~ Rosie Jane Lofton ~ Karen Scott ~ Diane Campbell ~ Bobbie Hayes-Johnson

Florence Mathis Butler ~ Corrine V. West ~ Lee Eloise Smith ~ Linda Hargrove ~ Lana Long

Connie Smith ~ Sheila Zinnerman ~ Monica Haynes ~ Doranna Tyler ~ Bessie Jean Manga ~ Mesnelle Jean-Mary

Table of Contents

Prompted Journal

A place for your thoughts when you pick up the phone
to tell her something...

_____

_____

_____

_____

_____

_____

_____

_____

_____

_____

_____

_____

A place for your thoughts when you really want to spend some time with her...

_____

_____

_____

_____

_____

_____

_____

_____

_____

_____

_____

A place for your thoughts when you need her advice and guidance...

_____

_____

_____

_____

_____

_____

_____

_____

_____

_____

_____

A place for your thoughts when you wish you had a chance to apologize ...

_____

_____

_____

_____

_____

_____

_____

_____

_____

_____

_____

A place for your thoughts when the lessons she taught you become relevant ...

_____

_____

_____

_____

_____

_____

_____

_____

_____

_____

_____

A place for your thoughts when you reach goals that you and Mommy talked about...

_____

_____

_____

_____

_____

_____

_____

_____

_____

_____

A place for your thoughts when you see something that reminds you of her...

_____

_____

_____

_____

_____

_____

_____

_____

_____

_____

_____

A place for your thoughts when you begin to face
your own mortality...

_____

_____

_____

_____

_____

_____

_____

_____

_____

_____

_____

A place for your thoughts when you are angry she left you alone...

_____

_____

_____

_____

_____

_____

_____

_____

_____

_____

_____

A place for your thoughts when you dream of her...

_____

_____

_____

_____

_____

_____

_____

_____

_____

_____

_____

_____

Stories about Mom I don't want to forget...

_____

_____

_____

_____

_____

_____

_____

_____

_____

_____

_____

Freeform Journal

Mommy's Meals

This is a place for you to jot down the family recipes and secrets so that fix—all soup or hometown macaroni and cheese will not be lost!

You can hold mommy close to your heart, and still pass her along in rich traditions of family and food while still fostering healing!

recipe:_____

ingredients:

_____ _____
_____ _____
_____ _____
_____ _____
_____ _____

directions:

_____
_____
_____
_____
_____
_____
_____
_____
_____
_____

recipe:_____

ingredients:

_____ _____
_____ _____
_____ _____
_____ _____
_____ _____

directions:

_____
_____
_____
_____
_____
_____
_____
_____
_____
_____

recipe:_____

ingredients:

_____ _____
_____ _____
_____ _____
_____ _____
_____ _____

directions:

_____
_____
_____
_____
_____
_____
_____
_____
_____
_____

recipe:_____

ingredients:

_____ _____
_____ _____
_____ _____
_____ _____
_____ _____

directions:

_____
_____
_____
_____
_____
_____
_____
_____
_____
_____

recipe:_____

ingredients:

_____ _____

_____ _____

_____ _____

_____ _____

_____ _____

directions:

_____

_____

_____

_____

_____

_____

_____

_____

_____

_____

_____

recipe:_____

ingredients:

_____ _____

_____ _____

_____ _____

_____ _____

_____ _____

directions:

_____

_____

_____

_____

_____

_____

_____

_____

_____

_____

_____

recipe:_____

ingredients:

_____ _____
_____ _____
_____ _____
_____ _____
_____ _____

directions:

_____
_____
_____
_____
_____
_____
_____
_____
_____
_____
_____

recipe:_____

ingredients:

_____ _____
_____ _____
_____ _____
_____ _____
_____ _____

directions:

_____
_____
_____
_____
_____
_____
_____
_____
_____
_____
_____

recipe:_____

ingredients:

_____ _____
_____ _____
_____ _____
_____ _____
_____ _____

directions:

_____
_____
_____
_____
_____
_____
_____
_____
_____
_____

73

recipe:_____

ingredients:

_____ _____
_____ _____
_____ _____
_____ _____
_____ _____

directions:

_____
_____
_____
_____
_____
_____
_____
_____
_____
_____

recipe:_____

ingredients:

_____ _____

_____ _____

_____ _____

_____ _____

_____ _____

directions:

_____

_____

_____

_____

_____

_____

_____

_____

_____

_____

recipe:_____

ingredients:

_____ _____

_____ _____

_____ _____

_____ _____

_____ _____

directions:

_____

_____

_____

_____

_____

_____

_____

_____

_____

_____

recipe:_____

ingredients:

_____ _____
_____ _____
_____ _____
_____ _____
_____ _____

directions:

_____
_____
_____
_____
_____
_____
_____
_____
_____
_____

recipe:_____

ingredients:

_____ _____
_____ _____
_____ _____
_____ _____
_____ _____

directions:

_____
_____
_____
_____
_____
_____
_____
_____
_____
_____

recipe:_____

ingredients:

_____ _____
_____ _____
_____ _____
_____ _____
_____ _____

directions:

_____
_____
_____
_____
_____
_____
_____
_____
_____
_____

recipe:_____

ingredients:

_____ _____
_____ _____
_____ _____
_____ _____
_____ _____

directions:

_____
_____
_____
_____
_____
_____
_____
_____
_____
_____

(PHOTO HERE)

MY MOMMY

·